# UNVEILING JOHN WICK:

## UNLEASHING THE BABA YAGA

---

### AN IN-DEPTH ANALYSIS AND ANATOMY OF A MODERN ACTION HERO

-

CREATED BY

# ETERNIA PUBLISHING

Unveiling John Wick: Unleashing The Baba Yaga: An In-Depth
Analysis And Anatomy Of A Modern Action Hero
By Eternia Publishing and Zander Pearce



Author: Eternia Publishing and Zander Pearce
Contact: contact@eterniapublishing.com

# CONTENT

# INTRODUCTION

**"Unveiling John Wick: Unleashing The Baba Yaga: An In-Depth Analysis And Anatomy Of A Modern Action Hero"** is a comprehensive exploration of the highly acclaimed action movie franchise starring Keanu Reeves as the legendary assassin, John Wick. This book aims to delve deep into the cinematic world of John Wick, analyzing various aspects of the film such as the action sequences, the use of color, and the significance of characters and their relationships.

Throughout the following chapters, readers will learn about John Wick's fighting style and the intricacies of the combat scenes. The emotional journey of John Wick will be explored, including themes of revenge, redemption, and his relationship with his past.

The roles of women and key characters such as Winston and the Adjudicator will be analyzed in depth, providing a more comprehensive understanding of the world of John Wick. Additionally, readers will learn about the significance of the Continental's global network, the role of New York City, and the influence of classic cinema on the franchise.

Furthermore, the book will examine the practical effects, the use of sound, and the title sequence of John Wick. The symbolism of John Wick's tattoos and the importance of the number 111 will also be explored.

Finally, the book concludes with a look at John Wick's legacy and the impact it has had on the action genre.

**"Unveiling John Wick: Unleashing The Baba Yaga: An In-Depth Analysis And Anatomy Of A Modern Action Hero"** offers a detailed and comprehensive analysis of the film, exploring its various aspects in great depth. It provides a deeper understanding of the film's themes, characters, and cinematic elements, making it a must-read for fans of the franchise and cinema enthusiasts alike.

# THE ORIGINS OF JOHN WICK

Are shrouded in mystery, but the events that led to his transformation into the legendary assassin we see on screen are rooted in tragedy.

John Wick, played by Keanu Reeves, was once a hitman for the Russian mafia, known as the "Boogeyman" due to his reputation for being the most efficient and deadly killer in the business. However, before he became the feared assassin, he had a happy life with his wife, Helen.

Helen was everything to John, and their love was the center of his world. Unfortunately, Helen fell ill with an undisclosed illness, and despite his best efforts and medical treatments, she passed away. John was devastated, and the world he knew crumbled around him.

To add to his misery, John received a posthumous gift from Helen in the form of a puppy. This puppy was a symbol of Helen's love for John and a way to help him cope with her loss. The puppy was the last connection to his wife, and John found solace in caring for the animal.

However, John's grief would not be given a chance to run its course. One day, Iosef Tarasov, the son of Viggo Tarasov, the head of the Russian mafia, broke into John's house, stole his car, and killed his puppy. The puppy, a symbol of hope and love, was the last straw for John, and his grief turned to rage.

This act of senseless violence was the catalyst that set John on a path of destruction, seeking vengeance against the people who killed his beloved pet. He returned to his former life as a hitman and took on the entire Russian mafia to avenge his dog's death. His mission was not just about the puppy, but about honoring the memory of his beloved wife, whose love for him had been betrayed by the Tarasov family.

Throughout his journey, John showcases his skills as a deadly assassin. From his impeccable aim to his hand-to-hand combat abilities, John proves that he is the Boogeyman that everyone fears. However, the John Wick we see in the film is not just a killing machine. He has a moral code, and his actions are guided by a sense of justice that goes beyond personal vendettas.

In the end, John's quest for vengeance leads him to confront Viggo, who is also Iosef's father. Viggo tries to bargain with John, offering him his life and the lives of his men in exchange for his own. John rejects the offer and engages in a final showdown with Viggo, which he wins.

The events that led to John Wick's transformation into the Boogeyman were tragic, but they showed us a different side to the character. John's vulnerability and pain made him more human, and his quest for vengeance made him relatable. His code of ethics and sense of justice added depth to his character, and his proficiency as a killer made him formidable.

The origins of John Wick show us that sometimes, it takes a tragedy to bring out the best (and worst) in people. John's journey was one of pain, grief, and ultimately, redemption. His story is a testament to the human spirit and the lengths people will go to when they are pushed beyond their limits. John Wick is more than just a killing machine; he is a complex character with a rich backstory that makes him one of the most compelling action heroes of our time.

# THE SECRET WORLD OF ASSASSINS

The world of assassins depicted in the John Wick films is a dark and secret one, hidden from the view of ordinary society. It is a world where people live and die by the code of the underworld, where honor and loyalty are valued above all else. This chapter explores the intricacies of this hidden world and how it affects the characters in the film.

Assassins in the world of John Wick operate under a set of rules and codes that govern their actions. These rules are enforced by an organization known as the High Table, which oversees the world of assassins and ensures that its members abide by the codes. The High Table is an unseen entity, operating behind the scenes to maintain order and control. Its members are powerful and influential figures in the underworld, and their word is law.

One of the most important rules in the world of assassins is the concept of the "marker." A marker is a blood oath that one assassin makes to another, and it is considered sacred. If an assassin accepts a marker, they are bound to complete the task assigned to them, no matter the cost. In the first John Wick film, the marker that John is given by Santino D'Antonio sets off a chain of events that leads to the death and destruction that follows.

Another key feature of the world of assassins is the concept of "continental rules." The Continental is a hotel that serves as a sanctuary for assassins, and it is also neutral ground where no violence is allowed.

The rules of the Continental dictate that no killing can take place on its premises, and anyone who violates this rule is excommunicado, or cast out from the world of assassins. In the films, the Continental is a central location where many of the key scenes take place, and it serves as a reminder that even in the underworld, there are still rules that must be followed.

The world of assassins in John Wick is also characterized by its unique sense of honor and loyalty. Assassins are expected to uphold a certain standard of behavior, and those who fail to do so are punished severely. In the second film, when Cassian, the bodyguard of Santino D'Antonio, disobeys his orders, he is disciplined by the High Table and forced to pay a steep price for his failure. This sense of honor and loyalty is also evident in John's relationship with his mentor, Winston, who runs the Continental. Although they are on opposite sides of the conflict in the films, they share a deep respect for each other and a code of honor that governs their actions.

Finally, the world of assassins in John Wick is one that is constantly changing and evolving. New players enter the scene, and old alliances are broken. In the third film, we see the introduction of the Adjudicator, a representative of the High Table who is tasked with punishing those who have broken the rules. The Adjudicator is a reminder that even in the world of assassins, there are those who hold power over others, and those who defy them do so at their own peril.

The secret world of assassins depicted in the John Wick films is a complex and intricate one. Its members are bound by codes and rules that govern their actions, and those who violate them are punished severely. The world of assassins is one of honor and loyalty, where alliances are constantly shifting, and new players enter the scene. Although it is a world of violence and death, it is also a world where relationships and respect are valued, and where even the most ruthless killers have a code that they live by.

# A LOOK INTO
# THE CONTINENTAL HOTEL

The Continental Hotel is a central location in the John Wick films, serving as a sanctuary for assassins and a hub for the criminal underworld. It is a place where the rules of the High Table are strictly enforced, and where even the most dangerous killers must abide by a certain code of conduct. This chapter explores the significance of the Continental Hotel and its role in the world of John Wick.

The Continental is more than just a hotel. It is a safe haven for assassins, a neutral ground where no violence is allowed. The rules of the Continental are enforced by its manager, Winston, who is a respected figure in the criminal underworld. The hotel is a place where assassins can come to rest, relax, and even make business deals with each other, knowing that they are safe from harm.

One of the most significant aspects of the Continental is the code of conduct that all visitors must abide by. No killing is allowed on the premises, and anyone who violates this rule is excommunicado, or cast out from the world of assassins. This rule is strictly enforced, as we see in the first film when John Wick kills a man in the hotel, leading to his excommunication and the start of his violent quest for revenge.

The Continental is also home to a number of unique services and amenities that cater to the needs of its clientele. These include a bar, a restaurant, a tailor, and a concierge service. The bar is a popular spot for assassins to gather and socialize, while the restaurant offers fine dining for those looking for a more formal experience.

The tailor is known for his impeccable suits, which are often worn by assassins during their jobs. The concierge service is particularly noteworthy, as it provides assassins with access to a wide range of resources and contacts, making it an essential tool for those operating in the criminal underworld.

Another interesting aspect of the Continental is the mysterious room known as the "sommelier's vault." This room is off-limits to all but a select few, and it is said to contain an array of deadly weapons and other items that can be used in assassinations. The sommelier's vault is a reminder of the dangerous and unpredictable nature of the world of assassins, and of the fact that even in the relative safety of the Continental, danger is always lurking.

The design and decor of the Continental are also significant. The hotel is characterized by its elegant and sophisticated atmosphere, with dark wood paneling, plush carpets, and ornate furnishings. The overall effect is one of luxury and refinement, with a touch of danger lurking just beneath the surface. The Continental is a visually striking location, and it serves as a powerful symbol of the world of assassins and the glamour that can come with a life of crime.

The Continental Hotel is a central location in the world of John Wick, serving as a safe haven for assassins and a hub for the criminal underworld. It is a place where the rules of the High Table are strictly enforced, and where even the most dangerous killers must abide by a certain code of conduct. The hotel is characterized by its elegant and sophisticated atmosphere, with a touch of danger lurking just beneath the surface. The Continental is a reminder that even in the world of assassins, there are rules and codes of conduct that must be followed, and that danger is always just around the corner.

# THE IMPORTANCE
# OF GOLD COINS

In the world of John Wick, gold coins are a universal currency that plays a significant role in the economy of the criminal underworld. These coins are highly valued by assassins and other criminals, and they are used to buy everything from weapons and ammunition to lodging and transportation. This chapter explores the importance of gold coins in the world of John Wick.

Gold coins are an essential element of the criminal economy in the John Wick films. They are used to buy and sell goods and services within the criminal underworld, and they are accepted by almost every criminal organization in the world. Assassins use gold coins to pay for their weapons, ammunition, and other supplies, and they are also used to pay for lodging and transportation. In essence, gold coins are the lifeblood of the criminal underworld, allowing its members to buy and sell goods and services without the use of traditional currencies.

One of the most significant aspects of gold coins is their universality. They are accepted by almost every criminal organization in the world, regardless of its location or affiliations. This universality is due in part to the fact that gold is a valuable and widely recognized commodity, but it is also due to the fact that the coins themselves are highly regulated by the High Table, the governing body of the criminal underworld. The High Table ensures that the coins are of a certain quality and weight, and it monitors their circulation to prevent counterfeiting and other forms of fraud.

Another important aspect of gold coins is their ability to buy loyalty and trust. In the world of John Wick, loyalty is a rare and valuable commodity, and assassins are often willing to do almost anything to gain it.

By offering gold coins as payment, assassins can buy the loyalty of others, whether it be a fellow assassin, a hotel manager, or a taxi driver. This creates a network of trust and cooperation within the criminal underworld, allowing its members to work together more effectively.

The use of gold coins also has symbolic significance in the world of John Wick. The coins themselves are highly stylized, with intricate designs and symbols that are rich in meaning. The coins represent power, wealth, and prestige, and they are a symbol of membership in the world of assassins. The fact that they are made of gold also gives them a sense of permanence and durability, emphasizing the importance of the criminal economy in the world of John Wick.

One of the most interesting aspects of gold coins is their ability to reveal information about the world of John Wick. As we see in the films, the coins often have different markings or symbols that can be used to identify their origin or affiliation. This provides insight into the complex web of relationships that exists within the criminal underworld, and it highlights the importance of reputation and alliances in this world. The coins also reveal the degree of organization and regulation that exists within the world of assassins, emphasizing the role of the High Table in maintaining order and stability.

Gold coins are a highly important element of the criminal economy in the world of John Wick. They serve as a universal currency that is accepted by almost every criminal organization in the world, and they are used to buy and sell goods and services within the criminal underworld. Gold coins are also highly symbolic, representing power, wealth, and prestige, and they reveal important information about the world of John Wick and its complex web of relationships. Ultimately, gold coins are a key element of the world-building in the John Wick films, emphasizing the importance of the criminal economy and its role in shaping the lives of the characters.

# JOHN WICK'S FIGHTING STYLE

One of the most striking elements of the John Wick films is the incredible fighting style displayed by the titular character. John Wick's fighting style is fast, brutal, and highly effective, allowing him to take on multiple opponents at once and emerge victorious. In this chapter, we will explore the key elements of John Wick's fighting style and the real-world martial arts techniques that inspire it.

First and foremost, John Wick's fighting style is characterized by its speed and agility. Wick is a highly skilled martial artist, and his movements are fluid and precise. He is able to quickly move from one opponent to the next, striking with deadly accuracy and evading attacks with ease. This agility is due in part to Wick's extensive training in Brazilian Jiu-Jitsu, a grappling-based martial art that emphasizes fluid movement and leverage.

Another key element of Wick's fighting style is his use of firearms. Wick is a highly skilled marksman, and he is able to shoot with deadly accuracy even in the midst of intense combat. He is also highly skilled at reloading and clearing malfunctions, allowing him to stay in the fight even when his ammunition runs low. This skill with firearms is a reflection of Wick's background as a hitman, and it gives him a significant advantage over his opponents.

Perhaps the most distinctive element of Wick's fighting style is his use of close-quarters combat. Wick is a master of hand-to-hand combat, and he is able to take down opponents with a variety of strikes and grappling techniques. His use of Judo and Jiu-Jitsu allows him to take advantage of his opponent's movements and leverage their weight against them. He is also highly skilled at using improvised weapons, such as pencils and books, to deadly effect.

Wick's fighting style is heavily influenced by the martial arts of Brazil, particularly Brazilian Jiu-Jitsu and Judo. These martial arts emphasize leverage and grappling, and they are highly effective in close-quarters combat. The choreography of the fight scenes in the John Wick films also incorporates elements of Muay Thai, a striking-based martial art from Thailand. This combination of grappling and striking techniques gives Wick a highly diverse fighting style that is well-suited to taking on multiple opponents at once.

It is worth noting that Wick's fighting style is highly efficient and practical. He does not waste movements or strikes, instead focusing on techniques that are highly effective and can quickly incapacitate his opponents. This efficiency is a reflection of Wick's background as a hitman, where every action must be calculated and precise.

John Wick's fighting style is a highly effective combination of Brazilian Jiu-Jitsu, Judo, and Muay Thai. He is able to take on multiple opponents at once with a combination of speed, agility, and deadly accuracy. Wick's use of firearms and improvised weapons adds an additional layer of danger to his fighting style, and his efficiency and practicality make him a formidable opponent. The fight scenes in the John Wick films are a testament to the skill and creativity of the choreographers, and they showcase the incredible fighting style of one of cinema's most memorable characters.

# AN ANALYSIS
# OF THE ACTION SEQUENCES

The John Wick franchise is renowned for its pulse-pounding, expertly choreographed action sequences. These scenes are a highlight of the films, showcasing the incredible skills of the character of John Wick and the creative talents of the filmmakers. In this chapter, we will analyze the action sequences of the John Wick films and examine the techniques and strategies employed to create some of the most exciting and memorable fight scenes in recent cinema.

One of the most striking aspects of the action sequences in the John Wick films is their realism. Unlike many Hollywood action movies, the John Wick franchise avoids the use of obvious CGI effects and wire work, opting instead for practical stunts and fight choreography. This gives the scenes a grittiness and immediacy that is often missing from other action films.

The fight scenes in the John Wick films are heavily choreographed, with a focus on timing and precision. The filmmakers use a variety of techniques to create visually stunning and dynamic sequences. One technique frequently used is long takes, where the camera follows the action without cutting. This allows the audience to fully appreciate the movements and choreography of the fight scenes and creates a sense of tension and excitement.

Another key element of the fight scenes in the John Wick films is the use of a wide range of weapons. From guns and knives to pencils and books, John Wick uses whatever is at his disposal to take down his opponents. This adds a level of creativity and unpredictability to the fight scenes, and allows the filmmakers to create unique and memorable moments.

The fight scenes in the John Wick films are also characterized by a sense of physicality. The filmmakers emphasize the impact of the strikes and blows, with sound effects and visual cues making it clear when a hit lands. This adds a level of realism to the fight scenes, and makes them more visceral and engaging for the audience.

One of the most notable aspects of the action sequences in the John Wick franchise is the way they are shot and edited. The filmmakers use a variety of camera angles and editing techniques to create a sense of movement and dynamism in the fight scenes. Quick cuts and fast-paced editing create a sense of urgency and excitement, while slow-motion shots allow the audience to fully appreciate the choreography and impact of the fight scenes.

The use of sound is also a key element of the action sequences in the John Wick films. The filmmakers use a range of sound effects to create a sense of impact and intensity, from the sound of gunshots to the thud of bodies hitting the ground. This adds an additional layer of realism and engagement to the fight scenes, immersing the audience in the action.

The action sequences in the John Wick films are a testament to the skill and creativity of the filmmakers and choreographers. They are characterized by their realism, physicality, and dynamic choreography, and employ a range of techniques to create some of the most exciting and memorable fight scenes in recent cinema. The filmmakers use a variety of camera angles, editing techniques, and sound effects to create a sense of movement and urgency, and the use of a wide range of weapons and improvised objects adds an element of creativity and unpredictability to the scenes. The action sequences in the John Wick films are a highlight of the franchise, and are sure to be remembered as some of the most thrilling and well-executed fight scenes in modern cinema.

# THE USE OF COLOR IN THE FILM

The use of color in filmmaking is an essential tool for directors to communicate themes, emotions, and ideas to the audience. The John Wick franchise is no exception, with its filmmakers using color in a deliberate and purposeful way to enhance the story and the characters. In this chapter, we will analyze the use of color in the John Wick films and examine how it contributes to the overall visual style of the franchise.

One of the most striking aspects of the John Wick films is their distinct visual style, which is characterized by a muted color palette and a focus on shadow and contrast. The films utilize a lot of dark, moody blues and greens, which create an eerie and unsettling atmosphere. This is particularly evident in scenes set in the Continental Hotel, where the blue lighting creates a sense of secrecy and danger.

Another color that features prominently in the John Wick films is red. The color red is often associated with violence, passion, and intensity, and the filmmakers use it to great effect in the fight scenes. Blood is a recurring visual motif throughout the franchise, with the red color adding a sense of brutality and danger to the action sequences.

The filmmakers also use color to differentiate between different characters and factions in the films. For example, the assassins of the Continental Hotel are often dressed in black and white, which creates a sense of formality and professionalism. In contrast, the character of Santino D'Antonio wears a lot of red, which is indicative of his violent and unpredictable nature.

Color is also used to communicate emotional states and character arcs. In John Wick: Chapter 2, the character of Cassian wears a blue suit throughout the film. However, after his fight with John Wick in the catacombs, his suit becomes increasingly stained with blood, and the blue color fades away. This communicates his descent into violence and sets up his character arc for the rest of the film.

In addition to the use of color in the film itself, the John Wick franchise also utilizes color in its marketing and promotional material. The iconic poster for the first film features a stark black background with a white silhouette of John Wick and a red line of blood, encapsulating the film's style and themes in a simple and striking image.

The use of color in the John Wick films is a testament to the filmmakers' attention to detail and their commitment to creating a distinct and memorable visual style. By using color to communicate themes, emotions, and ideas, the films are able to convey a sense of atmosphere and mood that enhances the story and the characters. From the muted blues and greens to the bold reds and blacks, the colors of the John Wick franchise are an integral part of its visual language and are sure to be remembered as one of the defining elements of the series.

# JOHN WICK'S EMOTIONAL JOURNEY

While the John Wick franchise is perhaps best known for its exhilarating action sequences, it is also a story about a man grappling with grief, loss, and the desire for vengeance. In this chapter, we will explore John Wick's emotional journey throughout the series and examine how it informs his character and actions.

The first film begins with John Wick as a grieving widower, mourning the loss of his beloved wife Helen. It is revealed that Helen was the one bright spot in an otherwise violent and bloody life, and her death has left John with nothing but memories and a sense of emptiness. The film sets up John's emotional journey by establishing the depth of his grief and the lengths he will go to in order to seek revenge against those who have wronged him.

As the series progresses, we see John grappling with the consequences of his actions and the toll that his quest for revenge has taken on his psyche. He is haunted by the memories of those he has killed and struggles to find a sense of purpose beyond his thirst for vengeance. In John Wick: Chapter 2, he is forced to honor a debt to the Italian mob, leading him on a path of violence and betrayal that culminates in the death of his closest friend.

The third film, John Wick: Chapter 3 - Parabellum, sees John pushed to his limits as he becomes a target of the High Table, the governing body of the world's assassins. He is forced to confront his own mortality and the reality that his actions have consequences, not only for himself but for those he cares about. The film ends with John seemingly alone and on the run, setting up the emotional stakes for the next installment of the franchise.

Throughout the series, John's emotional journey is marked by a sense of loneliness and isolation. He is a man who has lost everything and has only his thirst for revenge to keep him going. However, he is also a man who is capable of love and compassion, as seen in his relationships with his dog and his fellow assassins.

Perhaps the most poignant moment of John's emotional journey comes in the third film, when he visits the Continental Hotel and is reunited with his old mentor, Winston. The two men share a moment of genuine connection, with Winston acknowledging the depth of John's pain and offering him a chance at redemption. It is a moment of vulnerability for John, who is forced to confront the reality of his situation and the consequences of his actions.

John's emotional journey is one of redemption and self-discovery. He is a man who has been consumed by his grief and his thirst for revenge, but who is also capable of finding a sense of purpose beyond his violent past. The franchise's final film, John Wick: Chapter 4, promises to bring John's emotional journey to a close, offering a chance for him to find peace and closure in a world that has brought him nothing but pain and bloodshed.

John Wick's emotional journey is an integral part of the franchise's narrative and character development. By exploring his grief, loss, and desire for vengeance, the films offer a compelling portrait of a man struggling to come to terms with his past and find a sense of purpose in a violent and chaotic world. The emotional stakes of John's journey lend a depth and nuance to the action sequences, making them all the more thrilling and impactful. As the franchise continues to evolve, we can only hope that John's journey will continue to be a central focus, offering a chance for audiences to explore the complexities of the human experience through the lens of a modern-day action hero.

# THE THEMES OF
# REVENGE AND REDEMPTION

The John Wick franchise is built on a foundation of revenge and redemption, two themes that run throughout the series and inform the actions of its eponymous protagonist. In this chapter, we will explore these themes and how they are used to create a compelling and emotionally resonant narrative.

Revenge is perhaps the most obvious and overt theme of the John Wick franchise. The films are built around the concept of a man seeking vengeance for the wrongs that have been done to him. John's quest for revenge begins with the death of his beloved wife Helen, which sets him on a path of violence and bloodshed. He is a man consumed by his thirst for revenge, willing to do whatever it takes to bring those who have wronged him to justice.

However, the films also explore the consequences of revenge and the toll that it takes on those who seek it. John's quest for vengeance ultimately leads him down a path of self-destruction, forcing him to confront the reality of his situation and the consequences of his actions. Revenge is shown to be a hollow victory, one that ultimately brings more pain and suffering than satisfaction.

Redemption is a theme that runs parallel to revenge throughout the franchise. John's journey is one of redemption, a quest to find meaning and purpose beyond his thirst for revenge. He is a man grappling with the consequences of his violent past and seeking a chance at redemption, a chance to make amends for the pain and suffering he has caused.

Redemption is seen in John's relationships with those around him, particularly his dog and his fellow assassins. These relationships offer a glimpse into a man who is capable of love and compassion, even in the midst of violence and chaos. They also provide a sense of hope and optimism, offering the possibility of a future beyond the cycle of revenge and violence.

The films also explore the concept of redemption through the character of Winston, the owner of the Continental Hotel. Winston is a mentor figure to John, offering him guidance and support throughout his journey. He is a man who has found a sense of purpose beyond his violent past, serving as a protector and guardian of the assassins' community. Through his example, John is given a chance to find redemption and a sense of purpose beyond his quest for revenge.

The themes of revenge and redemption are used to create a complex and emotionally rich narrative, one that explores the depths of the human experience. The films offer a nuanced look at the consequences of violence and the toll that it takes on those who seek revenge. They also provide a sense of hope and optimism, offering the possibility of redemption and a chance for a better future.

The themes of revenge and redemption are central to the John Wick franchise, informing the actions of its eponymous protagonist and creating a compelling and emotionally resonant narrative. The films explore the consequences of revenge and the toll that it takes on those who seek it, while also offering a sense of hope and optimism through the concept of redemption. These themes lend a depth and complexity to the franchise, making it much more than a simple action movie. As the franchise continues to evolve, we can only hope that these themes will continue to be a central focus, offering a chance to explore the complexities of the human experience through the lens of a modern-day action hero.

# THE ROLE OF WOMEN IN JOHN WICK

The John Wick franchise has been praised for its portrayal of women, who are given prominent roles throughout the series. In this chapter, we will explore the role of women in the John Wick franchise, and how they contribute to the overall narrative.

One of the most notable aspects of the John Wick franchise is the presence of strong and capable female characters. These women are not simply relegated to the role of damsel in distress or love interest; they are given agency and agency and play an active role in the action and plot of the films.

Perhaps the most prominent female character in the franchise is Sofia, played by Halle Berry in John Wick: Chapter 3 – Parabellum. Sofia is a fellow assassin and former acquaintance of John's, who becomes an ally in his quest for vengeance. She is a highly skilled fighter, capable of taking down multiple opponents with ease. Her presence in the film offers a refreshing change from the male-dominated world of action cinema, and she is a welcome addition to the franchise.

Another significant female character is the Adjudicator, played by Asia Kate Dillon in John Wick: Chapter 3 – Parabellum. The Adjudicator is a high-ranking member of the High Table, the ruling council of the assassins' world. She is tasked with enforcing the rules and regulations of the High Table, and her presence adds a level of tension and conflict to the story. Dillon's performance is nuanced and understated, and the character is a fascinating addition to the franchise.

The role of women in the John Wick franchise is not limited to these two characters, however. Throughout the series, women are given prominent roles and agency. Even characters who appear briefly, such as the Bowery King's assistant, are given the opportunity to make an impact on the story. These women are not simply there to serve as eye candy or plot devices; they are fully realized characters with their own motivations and desires.

The presence of strong female characters in the John Wick franchise is a welcome change from the male-dominated world of action cinema. It offers a glimpse into a world where women are given agency and are capable of making a significant impact on the story. These characters serve as role models for young women, showing them that they too can be strong and capable in a world that often dismisses or belittles them.

The role of women in the John Wick franchise is an important aspect of the overall narrative. These characters are not simply there to serve as love interests or plot devices; they are fully realized and complex characters with their own motivations and desires. Their presence adds depth and complexity to the franchise, and offers a glimpse into a world where women are given agency and are capable of making a significant impact on the story. As the franchise continues to evolve, we can only hope that these strong and capable female characters will continue to be a central focus, offering a new perspective on the world of action cinema.

# THE CHARACTER OF WINSTON

In the John Wick franchise, Winston is a central character who serves as the manager of the Continental Hotel, a safe haven for assassins. In this chapter, we will explore the character of Winston, and how his actions and motivations contribute to the overall narrative of the series.

Winston is portrayed by Ian McShane, a veteran actor known for his captivating performances. McShane brings a sense of gravitas and wisdom to the role of Winston, making him a formidable and memorable character. Winston is a man of few words, but his actions speak volumes. He is a powerful figure in the world of assassins, and his position as manager of the Continental Hotel gives him considerable influence.

One of the most notable aspects of Winston's character is his loyalty to the Continental Hotel and its rules. The hotel is a neutral ground for assassins, and any violence committed on its premises is strictly forbidden. Winston is a staunch defender of the hotel's rules, and he will go to great lengths to ensure that they are upheld. This loyalty to the hotel and its rules is evident in his interactions with John Wick, who is forced to seek refuge at the hotel after being declared excommunicado.

Despite his loyalty to the hotel, Winston is not above making difficult decisions when necessary. In John Wick: Chapter 2, he gives John an impossible task, forcing him to take on a job that seems impossible to complete. This decision puts John's life in danger, but it is necessary to maintain the integrity of the hotel's rules. Winston's willingness to make difficult decisions demonstrates his commitment to the hotel's values, and adds depth and complexity to his character.

Winston is also a mentor figure to John, offering guidance and advice throughout the series. In John Wick: Chapter 2, he tells John, "You stabbed the devil in the back. To him, this isn't vengeance, this is justice." This line of dialogue encapsulates the central conflict of the series, and highlights the moral ambiguity that exists within the world of assassins. Winston's guidance offers insight into this complex world, and his presence serves as a reminder that there are consequences to every action.

Throughout the series, Winston is portrayed as a man of power and influence. His position as manager of the Continental Hotel gives him considerable authority, and he is able to command respect from even the most dangerous assassins. However, despite his power and influence, Winston is not invulnerable. In John Wick: Chapter 3 – Parabellum, he is shown to be vulnerable when he is attacked by the Adjudicator's forces. This moment of vulnerability serves as a reminder that even the most powerful figures in this world are not immune to danger.

The character of Winston is a central figure in the John Wick franchise. His loyalty to the Continental Hotel and its rules, his willingness to make difficult decisions, and his role as a mentor to John all contribute to the overall narrative of the series. Ian McShane's performance brings a sense of gravitas and wisdom to the character, making him a memorable and formidable presence. As the series continues to evolve, we can only hope that Winston's character will continue to be a central focus, offering insight into the complex world of assassins.

# THE ADJUDICATOR: AN ANALYSIS

In the John Wick series, the Adjudicator is a significant character who plays a pivotal role in the third installment, John Wick: Chapter 3 - Parabellum. The Adjudicator is portrayed by Asia Kate Dillon, and their character represents the High Table, a powerful organization that controls the world of assassins. In this chapter, we will analyze the Adjudicator's character and explore their significance in the John Wick universe.

The Adjudicator is a cold and calculating character who is tasked with maintaining order and enforcing the rules of the High Table. They are the face of the organization, and their word is law. The Adjudicator is a gender-nonconforming character who uses "they/them" pronouns, and this representation has been hailed as a progressive move by the filmmakers. The character's androgyny is symbolic of their power, and it serves to highlight their gender-neutral role in the High Table.

The Adjudicator is introduced in John Wick: Chapter 3 - Parabellum, and they are tasked with punishing those who have broken the High Table's rules. They are shown to be ruthless in their pursuit of justice and will stop at nothing to ensure that the rules are followed. The Adjudicator is seen meeting with the heads of various assassin clans, and they make it clear that those who have aided John Wick will face severe consequences.

Throughout the film, the Adjudicator is portrayed as a formidable opponent who is not to be underestimated. They are intelligent and resourceful, and they use their power to manipulate those around them. The Adjudicator is a master of psychological warfare, and they are adept at using fear and intimidation to achieve their goals.

One of the most striking aspects of the Adjudicator's character is their sense of honor. They believe that the rules of the High Table are sacrosanct and must be obeyed at all costs. They are willing to go to great lengths to maintain order and ensure that justice is served. The Adjudicator's sense of honor is juxtaposed with John Wick's code of ethics, which is based on personal loyalty and revenge.

The Adjudicator's character also serves to expand the lore of the John Wick universe. They provide insight into the inner workings of the High Table and offer a glimpse into the larger world of assassins. The Adjudicator's presence in the film creates a sense of tension and adds depth to the story.

The Adjudicator is a complex and fascinating character who plays a significant role in the John Wick series. Their character represents the High Table, and they are tasked with enforcing its rules. The Adjudicator's androgynous appearance is symbolic of their power and gender-neutral role. Their sense of honor and unwavering commitment to the rules of the High Table create a sense of tension and add depth to the story. The Adjudicator is a powerful addition to the John Wick universe, and their character serves to expand the lore of the series.

# THE CONTINENTAL'S GLOBAL NETWORK

The Continental Hotel is not just a luxurious accommodation for assassins, but it is also a part of a vast network that spans the entire globe. This network is what makes it possible for assassins to operate with relative ease and without fear of being caught by law enforcement. The global network of the Continental Hotel is a vital part of the John Wick universe and plays a significant role in the franchise's success.

The Continental is not just a hotel, but it is also an institution that provides a range of services for assassins. From transportation to weapons, the Continental can cater to almost any need of the assassins. The Continental's network extends beyond the walls of the hotel, and it includes numerous safe houses, drop-off points, and contacts across the globe.

The network is managed by the High Table, a group of powerful individuals who control the world of assassins. The High Table is responsible for enforcing the rules of the Continental, which includes a strict code of conduct that all assassins must adhere to. Failure to comply with the rules can lead to severe consequences, including excommunication, which means that the individual will be expelled from the network and will lose all privileges that come with being a part of it.

One of the most significant benefits of being a part of the Continental network is the use of gold coins. These coins are the currency of the assassins and are used to pay for goods and services within the network. They are also recognized as a form of payment outside the network, and many establishments accept them as payment.

The coins are valuable because they are untraceable, and they can be used to purchase almost anything, including weapons and favors.

The Continental's network extends beyond the United States, and it includes locations in Rome, Morocco, and New York City. The Continental hotel in New York City is one of the most prominent locations in the franchise and serves as the central hub for the network. It is the place where assassins from all over the world come to rest, recuperate, and conduct business.

The Continental network is essential for the John Wick franchise because it provides a sense of continuity throughout the movies. It ties together the various locations and characters, and it gives the audience a sense of the larger world that John Wick inhabits. The network also allows for the introduction of new characters and locations, which keeps the franchise fresh and exciting.

The Continental's global network is a vital part of the John Wick universe. It provides a range of services for assassins, including transportation, weapons, and safe houses. The network is managed by the High Table, and it includes numerous safe houses, drop-off points, and contacts across the globe. The use of gold coins is one of the most significant benefits of being a part of the network, and it allows for the purchase of almost anything. The Continental's network extends beyond the United States, and it includes locations in Rome, Morocco, and New York City. The network is essential for the franchise because it provides a sense of continuity throughout the movies, ties together the various locations and characters, and allows for the introduction of new characters and locations.

# THE SIGNIFICANCE
# OF THE MARKER

The Marker is a significant plot device in the John Wick universe, serving as a symbol of loyalty, obligation, and honor among assassins. In the first film, John Wick is called back into the world of violence when a group of Russian gangsters break into his home, steal his car, and kill his beloved dog. It is later revealed that the gangster who orchestrated the break-in, Iosef Tarasov, is the son of Viggo Tarasov, a powerful Russian mob boss who is also a member of the High Table, the governing body of the assassins' world.

To ensure that his son is safe from John Wick's wrath, Viggo invokes the Marker, a blood oath between him and John. This means that John is obligated to fulfill a task for Viggo in exchange for the favor Viggo did for John in the past. The Marker is a sacred tradition in the assassins' world, and breaking it is a serious offense that carries severe consequences.

The Marker serves as a symbol of honor and loyalty among assassins. It represents a debt owed to another person that can only be repaid through a task or favor. This bond is sacred and is respected by all members of the assassins' world. Failure to honor the Marker not only leads to severe consequences for the person who broke the bond but can also lead to a loss of reputation and standing in the world of assassins.

The Marker also plays a critical role in the second and third films, where it serves as the central plot device. In John Wick: Chapter 2, Santino D'Antonio, a member of the High Table, comes to John and asks him to fulfill a Marker. In exchange, Santino will use his influence to release John from his obligations to the assassins' world, allowing him to live a peaceful life once again. However, the Marker that Santino presents to John is an impossible task, leading to a series of events that thrust John back into the world of violence.

The Marker serves as a catalyst for the plot in John Wick: Chapter 3 - Parabellum, as the High Table places a bounty on John's head for breaking the rules of the assassins' world. Winston, the manager of the Continental Hotel, grants John a one-hour head start to escape the city, but he is then given a Marker by the Elder, a member of the High Table. The Marker is a symbol of the debt that John owes to the Elder, and he must fulfill the task given to him if he wants to be absolved of his sins and have his bounty lifted.

The Marker serves as a symbol of honor, loyalty, and obligation in the assassins' world. It is a sacred tradition that carries severe consequences if broken. The Marker also serves as a plot device in the John Wick films, driving the narrative and leading to a series of events that thrust John back into the world of violence. The Marker is a critical element of the John Wick universe, and it is a testament to the intricate world-building and attention to detail that goes into the making of these films.

# JOHN WICK'S RELATIONSHIP WITH HIS PAST

John Wick's past plays a significant role in the development of his character throughout the film franchise. From his background as a legendary hitman to the loss of his wife and the events that follow, John's past serves as a driving force for his actions and decisions.

John's history as an assassin is shrouded in mystery, with very few people aware of the extent of his skills and reputation. However, as the story progresses, we learn that John was once a part of a secret organization of assassins known as the High Table. He retired from the organization to start a new life with his wife, Helen, but her untimely death reignites his past and brings him back into the world he had left behind.

John's relationship with his past is complex, as he struggles to come to terms with the memories and trauma that he has repressed for years. Throughout the films, we see glimpses of his past through flashbacks and conversations with other characters, but it's not until the third installment, John Wick: Chapter 3 – Parabellum, that we are given a more in-depth look at his history.

In the film, John seeks help from Sofia, a fellow assassin and friend who owes him a debt. In exchange for her assistance, John gives her a "marker," which is a sign of debt owed between members of the High Table. This marker is a symbol of John's past and the debts he has accrued over his years as an assassin. It serves as a reminder of his former life, and the fact that he cannot escape his past.

John's journey throughout the films can be seen as a metaphor for the struggle to come to terms with one's past. He is haunted by memories of his wife and the guilt he feels for the actions he has taken as an assassin. His actions throughout the films can be seen as an attempt to reconcile his past and seek redemption for his sins.

The theme of redemption is particularly prevalent in the third installment, as John is given a chance to seek forgiveness for his actions by the Elder, a member of the High Table. The Elder offers John a chance to regain his status as a member of the High Table in exchange for killing Winston, the manager of the Continental Hotel. However, John chooses to spare Winston's life and instead goes on the run from the organization he once served.

Through his decision to spare Winston, John shows that he is no longer willing to blindly follow the rules of the High Table and that he is willing to make his own decisions. He has come to terms with his past and is now in control of his own fate.

John Wick's relationship with his past is a central theme throughout the film franchise. His struggles with his memories and guilt drive his actions, and his journey can be seen as a metaphor for the struggle to come to terms with one's past. The marker, a symbol of debt and obligation, serves as a reminder of John's former life and his inability to escape his past. However, through his actions and decisions, John shows that he is willing to seek redemption for his sins and forge his own path forward.

# THE ROLE OF NEW YORK CITY

The city of New York plays a significant role in the John Wick franchise. From the opening shots of the first film, it is clear that New York is more than just a backdrop for the action; it is a character in its own right. The city's iconic landmarks and gritty neighborhoods provide a rich and varied backdrop for John Wick's adventures, and the filmmakers take full advantage of their locations to create a unique and immersive experience for viewers.

One of the most striking aspects of the John Wick films is the way in which they depict New York as a dark and dangerous place. From the neon-lit streets of Times Square to the abandoned warehouses of Brooklyn, the city is portrayed as a seedy underworld of crime and corruption. This is reflected in the film's visual style, which is dominated by shades of black and gray. Even the rare moments of color, such as the golden glow of the Continental Hotel or the red of blood spilled in battle, serve to heighten the sense of danger and menace.

At the same time, however, the films also showcase the city's beauty and diversity. The sleek lines of the Chrysler Building, the lush greenery of Central Park, and the colorful characters who populate its streets all add to the richness of the film's visual palette. This contrast between the city's beauty and its darkness is a recurring theme throughout the franchise, and serves to highlight the complexity and nuance of the world John Wick inhabits.

Another key aspect of the role of New York in the John Wick films is the way in which the city is portrayed as a hub of international criminal activity. The Continental Hotel, with its network of assassins and underworld contacts, is just one example of the many ways in which the city serves as a meeting place for the world's most dangerous people. This sense of global connectivity is reinforced by the diverse range of accents and languages spoken by the characters, as well as by the film's use of international locations such as Rome and Casablanca.

Perhaps most importantly, however, New York serves as a metaphor for John Wick's own journey. As a former hitman who has tried to leave his violent past behind, John is haunted by memories of the city and the people he used to know. The film's flashbacks to John's life with his wife, as well as his interactions with old colleagues and enemies, serve to underscore this sense of nostalgia and regret. At the same time, however, the city also represents the possibility of redemption and renewal. Through his encounters with new allies such as the Bowery King and Sofia, as well as his quest to save his own life and the lives of those he cares about, John is able to carve out a new path for himself in the city he once called home.

The role of New York in the John Wick franchise is multifaceted and complex. From its depiction as a seedy underworld of crime and corruption to its portrayal as a hub of international activity, the city serves as a crucial element in the films' world-building and storytelling. More than that, however, New York also represents the personal journey of John Wick himself, as he grapples with his past, seeks redemption, and forges a new path forward. It is this blend of the personal and the universal that makes the city of New York such a compelling and integral part of the John Wick franchise.

# AN EXAMINATION OF THE SOUNDTRACK

Music is a crucial aspect of any film, and John Wick is no exception. The film's soundtrack, composed by Tyler Bates and Joel J. Richard, is an essential element of the movie's tone and atmosphere. The music works in conjunction with the visuals to create a heightened sense of tension, adrenaline, and drama.

The soundtrack is an eclectic mix of genres, combining electronic music, classical compositions, and rock and roll. The film's opening credits set the tone with Marilyn Manson's cover of "Sweet Dreams (Are Made of This)," providing a haunting and ominous introduction to the world of John Wick.

One of the most notable aspects of the soundtrack is its use of leitmotifs. A leitmotif is a recurring musical theme associated with a particular character, place, or concept. In John Wick, each character has their own distinct leitmotif that is repeated throughout the film.

The most recognizable leitmotif is associated with John Wick himself. The theme is introduced in the opening scene and is a driving force throughout the film. It consists of a simple piano melody that evolves into a full orchestral arrangement during the film's action sequences. The theme is a reflection of John Wick's character: stoic, determined, and relentless.

Other notable leitmotifs include those associated with the Continental Hotel, the Adjudicator, and the Bowery King. The Continental's leitmotif is a classical composition that emphasizes the hotel's luxurious and refined atmosphere. The Adjudicator's theme is ominous and tense, signifying her role as a formidable and intimidating presence.

The Bowery King's theme is a blend of electronic and rock music, reflecting his unconventional and rebellious nature.

The soundtrack also features a range of original songs, including "Think" by Kaleida, "Who You Talkin' To Man?" by Ciscandra Nostalghia, and "Killing Strangers" by Marilyn Manson. These songs provide an additional layer of intensity and energy to the film's action sequences.

Perhaps the most emotional moment of the film is when John Wick visits Aurelio's chop shop and hears "The Impossible Dream" by Andy Williams playing on the radio. The song's lyrics, which describe a quest for an unattainable goal, are a poignant reflection of John Wick's own journey. The song is also a nod to the film's references to classic literature and culture, as "The Impossible Dream" is a song from the musical Man of La Mancha, based on the novel Don Quixote.

The soundtrack is not only notable for its composition but also for its integration with the film's sound design. The music works in tandem with the sound effects to create a fully immersive experience. For example, during the nightclub sequence, the music and sound effects blend seamlessly, creating a chaotic and disorienting atmosphere.

The soundtrack of John Wick is an essential component of the film's success. The eclectic mix of genres, the use of leitmotifs, and the original songs all contribute to the film's atmosphere and intensity. The music serves as a reflection of the film's themes and characters, creating a fully realized world that immerses the audience in the story. It is a testament to the skill and talent of Tyler Bates and Joel J. Richard, and their contribution to the film's success should not be overlooked.

# JOHN WICK
# AND THE RUSSIAN MAFIA

John Wick's intense desire for revenge is triggered by the death of his beloved wife and the killing of his dog, a gift from his wife, by the Russian Mafia. The Russian Mafia plays a crucial role in the movie as it is the catalyst for John Wick's violent rampage.

The Russian Mafia is presented as an all-powerful and dangerous criminal organization that operates with impunity, controlling the city's criminal underworld. The movie's opening scenes introduce us to the leader of the Russian Mafia, Viggo Tarasov, a cold and calculating man who commands fear and respect from everyone around him.

Tarasov's relationship with John Wick is also established early in the movie. Wick is a former hitman who worked for Tarasov, and the two have a history. When Wick decides to leave the business to start a new life with his wife, Tarasov allows him to do so, but not before extracting a promise from Wick to perform a task for him in the future.

Wick's task is to kill Tarasov's own son, Iosef, who has stolen Wick's car and killed his dog. Tarasov knows that Wick is not a man to be trifled with and does everything in his power to protect his son from Wick's vengeance. However, as we see throughout the movie, Wick is a man on a mission, and nothing will stand in his way.

The movie's climax takes place in the Red Circle nightclub, where Wick faces off against Tarasov's henchmen in a brutal and bloody showdown. The scene is a masterpiece of action choreography and demonstrates Wick's unmatched skill and determination.

Throughout the movie, the Russian Mafia is portrayed as an organization that operates outside of the law, with its own rules and codes of conduct. It is a world that Wick knows intimately, having worked as a hitman for many years. The movie shows us how Wick's past catches up with him, forcing him to confront his own demons and his violent nature.

The Russian Mafia is also used as a symbol of the corrupting influence of power and money. We see this in the character of Viggo Tarasov, who is willing to do anything to protect his criminal empire, including sacrificing his own son. The movie suggests that the pursuit of power and wealth can lead to moral decay and the loss of one's humanity.

John Wick's relationship with the Russian Mafia is complex, and it is a testament to the movie's writing and storytelling that it can convey this complexity without the need for excessive exposition. The movie suggests that Wick's past with the Russian Mafia is something he is trying to escape, but at the same time, it is something that defines him.

The Russian Mafia is a crucial element of John Wick's world. It is a dangerous criminal organization that operates outside of the law, with its own rules and codes of conduct. The Russian Mafia is a symbol of the corrupting influence of power and money, and it plays a crucial role in the movie's plot. John Wick's relationship with the Russian Mafia is complex, and it is something that defines him and his violent nature. The Russian Mafia is one of the movie's most memorable and important aspects, and it is a testament to the movie's writing and storytelling that it can convey this importance without the need for excessive exposition.

# THE MEANING BEHIND JOHN WICK'S TATTOOS

In the film John Wick, the titular character is covered in tattoos, each with a significant meaning. These tattoos are not just random designs, but they represent his past and present life as an assassin. In this chapter, we will examine the meaning behind each tattoo and how they relate to John Wick's character.

The tattoo on John's back is the most prominent and well-known. It reads "Fortis Fortuna Adiuvat," which is a Latin phrase that means "Fortune Favors the Bold." This phrase represents John's determination and fearlessness in carrying out his duties as an assassin. John is not one to back down from a challenge and is always ready to face any situation head-on.

Another tattoo that stands out is the Russian lettering on John's left shoulder. The letters "Боже правый" transliterate to "Bozhe Pravyy," which roughly translates to "God is on the Right Side." This tattoo represents John's Russian heritage and his connection to his past life as a member of the Russian mafia.

On his right forearm, there is a tattoo of a woman's face surrounded by roses. This tattoo represents John's wife, Helen, who was taken from him by illness. The roses symbolize Helen's love for gardening and her passion for nature. This tattoo serves as a constant reminder of John's love for his wife and his loss.

There is also a tattoo of a cross with a vine wrapped around it on John's left shoulder. This tattoo is a nod to John's religious beliefs and represents his faith. The vine around the cross is a symbol of John's hope for new life after his wife's death.

On his left arm, there is a tattoo of a demon with wings, which represents the demon from the book of Revelations in the Bible. The tattoo symbolizes John's violent past as an assassin, and his willingness to do whatever it takes to get the job done.

Finally, on John's chest, there is a tattoo of a series of dots and lines, which is known as a tally mark. This tattoo represents the number of people John has killed throughout his career as an assassin. It is a constant reminder of the violence he has caused and the lives he has taken.

The tattoos on John Wick's body are not just random designs, but they represent his past and present life as an assassin. Each tattoo has significant meaning and serves as a constant reminder of the events that shaped him into the man he is today. From his determination to his faith, these tattoos tell the story of John Wick's life and his journey throughout the film.

# AN ANALYSIS
# OF THE TITLE SEQUENCE

The opening title sequence of "John Wick" is a masterful work of art that sets the tone for the entire film. Directed by David Leitch and Chad Stahelski, the sequence features a hauntingly beautiful score composed by Tyler Bates and Joel J. Richard. This chapter will provide an analysis of the title sequence, exploring its visual and musical elements and how they work together to create an unforgettable cinematic experience.

The sequence begins with a black screen, followed by the words "John Wick" in bold white letters. The letters are slightly raised, as if they are carved into stone, and the shadows they cast create a sense of depth and dimensionality. This effect is enhanced by the sound of a chisel striking stone, which underscores the importance and permanence of the title character's name.

Next, the screen fades to black again, and we hear the sound of a car engine revving up. The camera then cuts to a close-up of a muscle car's tailpipe, as the car drives down a deserted road at night. The sound of the engine is amplified, creating a visceral sensation of speed and power.

As the car drives past various neon signs, the camera lingers on each one for a few seconds, allowing us to take in the details. These signs advertise businesses such as "The Continental" and "The Red Circle," which we later learn are important locations in the film. The neon lights cast an eerie glow on the surrounding buildings, creating a sense of mystery and danger.

As the car drives through the city, we see glimpses of John Wick's past: his wedding, his wife's funeral, and his time spent with his beloved dog. These brief flashbacks are accompanied by the melancholy strains of Marilyn Manson's "Killing Strangers," which reinforces the sense of loss and grief that permeates the film.

The sequence then cuts to a close-up of John Wick's face, as he gazes intently into the camera. The camera lingers on his face for a few moments, allowing us to see the pain and anger etched into his features. This shot is accompanied by the sound of his breathing, which becomes increasingly heavy and labored.

The screen then fades to black again, and we hear the sound of a gun being cocked. When the screen returns, we see John Wick loading his gun with bullets, his face a mask of determination. The camera then cuts between shots of John Wick and shots of the city at night, with the sound of gunfire and explosions punctuating each edit. The visual and aural chaos of these shots create a sense of frenzied action and violence, foreshadowing the events that will unfold in the rest of the film.

Finally, the title sequence ends with the words "John Wick" in bold white letters again, followed by the tagline "Don't Set Him Off." This tagline encapsulates the film's central conflict, as John Wick is pushed to the brink of his capabilities by those who underestimate his skills and determination.

The title sequence of "John Wick" is a masterful example of visual and musical storytelling. Through its use of imagery, sound, and music, the sequence creates a sense of mood, tone, and character that sets the stage for the rest of the film. From the haunting score to the glimpses of John Wick's past to the frenzied action shots, every element of the sequence works together to create a cohesive and unforgettable cinematic experience.

# THE INFLUENCE OF CLASSIC CINEMA ON JOHN WICK

John Wick is a modern action film that stands out for its unique visual style and cinematic references to classic films. From its use of long takes to its emphasis on practical stunts, the film pays tribute to the action movies of the past while also blazing its own trail in the genre. In this chapter, we will explore the influence of classic cinema on John Wick.

One of the most obvious nods to classic cinema in John Wick is its use of long takes. The film's action sequences are often presented in extended, uninterrupted shots that allow the audience to fully appreciate the skill and athleticism of the actors and stunt performers. This technique is reminiscent of the long takes used in classic films such as Alfred Hitchcock's Rope and Stanley Kubrick's Paths of Glory.

Another aspect of John Wick that is influenced by classic cinema is its emphasis on practical stunts. Unlike many modern action films that rely heavily on computer-generated imagery (CGI), John Wick features real, physical stunts that are performed by the actors themselves. This commitment to practical effects harkens back to the golden age of action movies in the 1980s and 1990s, when films like Die Hard and Terminator 2: Judgment Day relied on practical stunts and effects to wow audiences.

The film's visual style is also heavily influenced by classic cinema. The use of bold, saturated colors and contrasting shadows in the film's lighting scheme is reminiscent of film noir, a genre of Hollywood cinema that emerged in the 1940s and was characterized by its moody atmosphere and stylized visuals. Similarly, the film's use of wide-angle lenses and deep focus shots gives it a classic Hollywood feel that is reminiscent of films like Citizen Kane and The Maltese Falcon.

In addition to its visual style, John Wick also features several overt references to classic cinema. For example, the film's main character, John Wick, is named after the American actor John Wayne, who was known for his tough-guy roles in Westerns and war movies. Similarly, the film's opening sequence features a clip from the classic 1962 film The Day the Earth Stood Still, which sets the tone for the film's blend of old and new.

Perhaps the most obvious reference to classic cinema in John Wick is its use of music. The film's soundtrack features a number of classic songs from the 1950s and 1960s, including "Le Castle Vania" by John Murphy, "Think" by Kaleida, and "Killing Strangers" by Marilyn Manson. These songs help to create a nostalgic atmosphere that is evocative of classic Hollywood films.

John Wick is a film that is deeply influenced by classic cinema. From its use of long takes and practical stunts to its visual style and overt references to classic films, the movie pays tribute to the history of action cinema while also innovating and pushing the genre forward. By drawing on the best elements of classic cinema and combining them with modern sensibilities, John Wick has created a unique cinematic experience that appeals to a wide range of audiences.

# THE USE OF PRACTICAL EFFECTS IN THE FILM

John Wick is a movie that is renowned for its use of practical effects. From the elaborate fight sequences to the numerous explosions, the film makes use of practical effects to create a visceral, real-world experience for its viewers. In this chapter, we will analyze the use of practical effects in John Wick and how they contributed to the film's success.

Practical effects are physical effects that are achieved using props, sets, and special effects makeup, rather than computer-generated imagery (CGI). John Wick's directors, Chad Stahelski and David Leitch, wanted to use practical effects as much as possible to make the action sequences look and feel realistic.

One of the most impressive practical effects in John Wick is the use of squibs. Squibs are small explosive devices that are attached to a person's body and are used to simulate bullet impacts. In John Wick, the squibs were used to great effect during the various gunfights, making each bullet impact look and feel real. The use of squibs helped to create a more immersive experience for the viewers and added to the film's gritty realism.

Another practical effect used extensively in the film was the use of practical stunts. The directors wanted to create a realistic and visceral experience for the viewers, so they opted to use real people and practical stunts as much as possible. This meant that actors were doing their own stunts and the filmmakers were using real vehicles and real explosions.

One of the most notable practical stunts in John Wick was the car chase scene. The filmmakers used a real car and real drivers to create the intense car chase sequence. This practical approach helped to make the chase sequence feel more realistic, and it was one of the most memorable scenes in the movie.

In addition to practical effects, the filmmakers also used special effects makeup to create realistic wounds and injuries. The use of practical effects makeup helped to add to the realism of the film, and it also allowed the actors to perform more dangerous stunts.

For example, during the nightclub fight sequence, John Wick is hit with a bottle, causing a large laceration on his face. This wound was created using practical effects makeup, and it looked incredibly realistic. The use of practical effects makeup helped to create a more immersive experience for the viewers, and it allowed the filmmakers to create more intense and visceral fight sequences.

The use of practical effects in John Wick helped to create a more realistic and immersive experience for the viewers. The filmmakers wanted the audience to feel like they were a part of the action, and the use of practical effects helped to achieve this goal. By using real people, real stunts, and real explosions, the filmmakers were able to create a film that felt grounded in reality, despite its over-the-top action sequences.

The use of practical effects in John Wick was a significant factor in the film's success. The directors' commitment to using practical effects helped to create a more realistic and immersive experience for the viewers, and it also allowed the actors to perform more dangerous stunts. From the use of squibs to the practical stunts and special effects makeup, the practical effects in John Wick helped to create a visceral and thrilling experience that audiences continue to enjoy.

# THE SIGNIFICANCE OF THE NUMBER 111

The number 111 appears multiple times throughout the John Wick franchise, and it has left many fans wondering about its significance. Some believe it is just a coincidence, while others believe it holds a deeper meaning. In this chapter, we will analyze the significance of the number 111 in the John Wick universe.

Firstly, the number 111 is prominently displayed on John Wick's back in the form of a tattoo. This tattoo is a marker of his former life as an assassin and his association with the High Table. It is revealed in the films that John Wick was once an elite member of the organization and that the tattoo was a badge of honor. However, as he tries to leave that life behind, the tattoo becomes a constant reminder of his past and his obligations to the organization. Therefore, the number 111 serves as a reminder of John Wick's past life and his struggle to leave it behind.

Secondly, the number 111 is seen multiple times in the Continental Hotel. For example, in the first film, John Wick is assigned Room 111, which is significant since it is the same room where he and his wife spent their honeymoon. The number 111 is also seen on the door of the room where the concierge, Charon, resides. In the second film, the code to access the secret elevator to the High Table is 111, and in the third film, the number 111 is seen on the keypad used to access the Continental's vault.

The use of the number 111 in the Continental Hotel is a way to show the audience the inner workings of the assassin underworld. It suggests that the Continental Hotel operates on a secret code and that only those who are part of the inner circle are privy to its secrets. Additionally, the number 111 may also be a symbol of the balance and order that the Continental Hotel represents. The three ones could represent the three rules of the Continental: no blood on Continental grounds, a marker must be honored, and no business can be conducted on Continental grounds.

Lastly, the number 111 may also be linked to the concept of Trinity in Christianity. The number 111 represents the Holy Trinity, which consists of the Father, the Son, and the Holy Spirit. This concept is further reinforced in the second film when John Wick seeks the help of the Bowery King, and they discuss the significance of the number 111. The Bowery King tells John Wick that "the only way out is through" and that "the Elder holds the key." This suggests that John Wick must go through a process of spiritual rebirth or redemption before he can truly escape his past.

The number 111 is a recurring symbol in the John Wick franchise, and its meaning may not be limited to a single interpretation. It may represent John Wick's past life as an assassin, the inner workings of the Continental Hotel, the balance and order of the assassin underworld, or even the concept of Trinity in Christianity. Whatever its true meaning may be, the use of the number 111 adds another layer of depth and complexity to the already rich and intricate world of John Wick.

# JOHN WICK: THE LEGACY

John Wick has become one of the most iconic characters in modern cinema, and his legacy is undeniable. In this chapter, we will explore the reasons behind his success, the impact he has had on the genre, and his influence on popular culture.

The character of John Wick was created by screenwriter Derek Kolstad, who drew inspiration from his own personal experiences and a number of classic films. However, it was the performance of Keanu Reeves that brought the character to life and made him a household name. Reeves, known for his roles in The Matrix and Speed, brought his trademark intensity and physicality to the role of John Wick, creating a character that was simultaneously brutal and vulnerable.

The success of John Wick can be attributed to several factors, including its unique blend of action, humor, and emotion. The film's expertly choreographed fight scenes, combined with its dark humor and poignant storyline, captured audiences' attention and made John Wick a hit.

Moreover, John Wick's success has had a significant impact on the action genre. The film's use of practical effects, intense fight sequences, and complex characters has set a new standard for action films. The success of John Wick has also inspired a number of imitators, many of which have failed to capture the same magic.

John Wick has also had a significant impact on popular culture, inspiring countless memes, merchandise, and even a video game. The character's signature look, including his tailored suits and slicked-back hair, has become an icon of style, and his infamous "pencil scene" has become a favorite among fans.

However, John Wick's legacy is not just limited to his impact on the action genre and popular culture. The character's journey has also resonated with audiences on a deeper level. John Wick's story is one of loss, grief, and redemption, and his struggle to come to terms with his past has struck a chord with viewers.

Moreover, John Wick's relationship with his dog, which is the catalyst for the entire film, has made him an unlikely hero and a symbol of hope in a world that can often be cruel and unfair. His unwavering loyalty and determination to protect his dog, even at the cost of his own life, has made him a hero to many.

John Wick's legacy is a testament to the power of great storytelling and iconic characters. The character's unique blend of action, humor, and emotion, combined with Keanu Reeves' unforgettable performance, has made him a true cinematic icon. Moreover, his impact on the action genre and popular culture, as well as his resonance with audiences on a deeper level, have cemented his place in film history.

# THE EVOLUTION OF JOHN WICK'S FIGHTING STYLE

The John Wick franchise has garnered immense popularity not just for its thrilling action sequences but also for its unique and sophisticated fighting style. John Wick's fighting style is a blend of various martial arts disciplines, firearms training, and tactical movements. In this chapter, we will explore the evolution of John Wick's fighting style over the course of the franchise and how it has contributed to the overall success of the films.

In the first John Wick movie, John primarily uses Brazilian Jiu-Jitsu, Judo, and Krav Maga to take down his opponents in close-quarters combat. He is also shown using his surroundings to his advantage, like using a pencil to take out one of his opponents. However, the fight choreography in the first movie is relatively straightforward, focusing on realism and practicality.

In John Wick: Chapter 2, the filmmakers introduced more complex and stylized fight sequences, incorporating elements from Japanese Jiu-Jitsu and Aikido. The fight scenes in this movie are more choreographed and stylized, with John using a variety of weapons like guns, knives, and even a pencil again.

The third installment of the franchise, John Wick: Chapter 3 – Parabellum, raised the bar even higher with its fight scenes. The filmmakers incorporated martial arts styles like Wing Chun and Capoeira, and also introduced more creative weapons like a book and a horse. The fight sequences in this movie are not only visually stunning but also emotionally engaging, as the audience is invested in John's journey and rooting for him to succeed.

One notable aspect of John's fighting style is his proficiency with firearms. In the first movie, he is shown using a variety of guns and tactical movements. In the subsequent movies, the filmmakers placed a greater emphasis on firearms training, with John shown reloading and clearing malfunctions with incredible speed and precision.

Another aspect of John's fighting style is his use of tactical movement. John is often seen using the environment to his advantage, like ducking behind cover or sliding under obstacles. He also incorporates tactical movements like the Mozambique Drill, which involves two shots to the chest and one to the head, into his fighting style.

The evolution of John Wick's fighting style is a testament to the dedication of the filmmakers and the performers involved in the franchise. The fight choreography in the movies is a blend of different martial arts styles, tactical movements, and firearm training, resulting in a unique and sophisticated fighting style that has become synonymous with the franchise.

John Wick's fighting style has evolved over the course of the franchise, becoming more complex, stylized, and emotionally engaging with each installment. The filmmakers have incorporated different martial arts disciplines, tactical movements, and firearms training to create a unique and sophisticated fighting style that has become one of the defining characteristics of the franchise.

# THE SYMBOLISM OF THE GOLD COINS

The gold coins in the John Wick franchise are a recurring symbol that holds significant meaning throughout the films. While the coins are used as currency in the world of assassins, they also serve a deeper symbolic purpose. In this chapter, we will explore the symbolism of the gold coins and what they represent in the world of John Wick.

The gold coins first appear in the first film, when John Wick is paying for his stay at the Continental hotel. The coins are presented in a luxurious case and are worth a significant amount of money, as they can be used to purchase a variety of services from the hotel. However, the coins also have a deeper significance in the world of assassins, as they represent honor and respect.

The use of gold coins as currency in the assassin world is symbolic of the way assassins operate outside of the normal laws and regulations of society. It also speaks to the idea of a hidden economy that exists within the world of organized crime. The use of these coins further reinforces the idea that the world of John Wick operates under a set of rules and codes that are unique to that world.

One of the most significant aspects of the gold coins is the fact that they are universally accepted throughout the world of assassins. No matter where John Wick goes, he can use these coins to purchase goods and services. This universality reinforces the idea of a shared culture and set of values among assassins.

Another symbolic aspect of the gold coins is their weight and heft. They are solid and tangible, which adds to their value and importance in the world of assassins. This weight also adds to the idea that the coins carry a certain level of honor and respect. The coins are not just a means of exchange; they represent a way of life and a set of values that are highly prized in the world of assassins.

The coins also serve as a form of identification. In the second film, John Wick presents a coin to a fellow assassin as a way of identifying himself and gaining access to the assassin's services. This reinforces the idea that the coins are not just a means of exchange, but also a way of communicating within the world of assassins.

In addition to their symbolic significance, the gold coins also serve as a plot device. In the third film, John Wick is forced to give up his coins as a form of punishment. This adds tension to the film and raises the stakes for John Wick as he attempts to regain his status and earn back his coins.

The gold coins in the John Wick franchise are a powerful symbol that represents honor, respect, and a shared set of values among assassins. The use of these coins reinforces the idea that the world of John Wick operates under a unique set of rules and codes that are distinct from the normal laws and regulations of society. The coins also serve as a form of identification and add tension to the plot of the films. the gold coins are a rich and complex symbol that adds depth and meaning to the world of John Wick.

# THE ROLE OF THE BOWERY KING

The Bowery King is a significant character in the John Wick franchise. He is a mysterious figure who operates from the underground world of New York City. His role in the franchise has become increasingly prominent, especially in the third installment, where he becomes a key ally of John Wick.

The Bowery King is played by actor Laurence Fishburne, who is best known for his roles in The Matrix and Hannibal. Fishburne's portrayal of the character adds depth and intrigue to the already complex story of John Wick.

One of the Bowery King's most significant contributions to the franchise is his knowledge of the underground world of New York City. He has connections to many of the other key players in the world of assassins, and he is often the first person John Wick turns to when he needs information or help.

The Bowery King also represents an alternative to the Continental, the organization that governs the world of assassins. While the Continental operates within a strict set of rules, the Bowery King is more of a free agent who is not bound by the same constraints. He represents a different kind of power and influence in the world of assassins.

The character of the Bowery King is also significant because of his relationship with John Wick. While the two characters are not always on the same side, they share a deep respect for each other. The Bowery King sees John Wick as a kind of kindred spirit, and he is willing to go to great lengths to help him when he needs it.

The Bowery King's backstory is another fascinating aspect of the character. It is revealed that he was once a powerful figure in the world of assassins but was betrayed and left for dead. He survived but was left with significant scars and a deep hatred for the people who betrayed him. This backstory adds depth to the character and helps to explain his motivations and actions throughout the franchise.

The Bowery King is a significant character in the John Wick franchise. His knowledge of the underground world of New York City, his relationship with John Wick, and his backstory all contribute to his importance. He represents an alternative to the Continental and adds depth and intrigue to the complex world of assassins.

# JOHN WICK AND THE MYTH OF THE LONE HERO

John Wick is a character that embodies the myth of the lone hero, a trope that has been present in literature and cinema for centuries. This chapter will explore how John Wick fits into this archetype and what this means for the character and the film franchise as a whole.

The lone hero is a character who operates outside of society's norms and laws. They are typically rugged, self-reliant, and have a strong sense of justice. They often have a tragic backstory, and their quest for vengeance or redemption drives their actions. In John Wick's case, his wife's death and the theft of his beloved car are the catalysts for his descent back into the world of violence and crime.

One of the defining characteristics of the lone hero is their reluctance to form close relationships or rely on others. This is evident in John Wick's interactions with other characters in the film. Despite having allies and acquaintances in the underworld, he remains emotionally distant and rarely shows vulnerability. His only true companion is his dog, whom he rescues and cares for after his wife's death. This bond serves as a reminder of John's humanity and the capacity for compassion that lies beneath his cold exterior.

Another key aspect of the lone hero is their moral code, which is often at odds with the laws and values of society. John Wick operates under a strict set of rules that govern the criminal underworld. His adherence to these codes sets him apart from other characters, such as his former employer, Viggo Tarasov, who values power and wealth above all else. John's refusal to compromise his values, even in the face of great danger, reinforces his status as a hero.

However, the myth of the lone hero is not without its flaws. While the character is often celebrated for their bravery and strength, they are also prone to isolation, depression, and burnout. John Wick's mental and physical state deteriorates over the course of the films, as he endures countless injuries and losses. His repeated confrontations with the criminal underworld take a toll on him, and he often appears exhausted and emotionally drained.

Furthermore, the lone hero is a problematic trope because it reinforces the idea that individuals can solve complex problems without the help of others or larger societal systems. It can also perpetuate a sense of exceptionalism and individualism that is at odds with more collective forms of action and change. While John Wick's actions are undeniably impressive, they cannot be seen as a sustainable solution to the problems that exist within his world.

John Wick's character fits squarely within the myth of the lone hero. He is a self-reliant, justice-seeking, and emotionally distant figure who operates outside of society's laws. While this archetype has its strengths, it also has its limitations and drawbacks. John's story serves as a reminder of the power of individual action but also underscores the need for more collective and systemic change.

# THE IMPORTANCE OF COSTUME DESIGN IN JOHN WICK

The costume design in John Wick plays a significant role in not only establishing the character of John Wick but also creating a unique world that feels both familiar and otherworldly. Costume designer Luca Mosca and his team worked closely with director Chad Stahelski to create a look for the film that was both stylish and practical, as well as reflective of the film's themes and motifs.

One of the most noticeable aspects of the film's costume design is the use of black clothing, particularly for John Wick. This choice not only gives Wick a sleek and sophisticated appearance but also reinforces the character's status as a mysterious and deadly assassin. The black clothing also serves to symbolize the film's overarching theme of death, which is evident in the film's dark and gritty tone.

However, the costume design also extends beyond the use of black clothing. The various characters in the film have unique looks that reflect their personalities and positions in the film's criminal underworld. For example, the character of Santino D'Antonio, a powerful mafia boss, is often seen wearing expensive suits and luxurious accessories, which reflect his wealth and power.

Additionally, the use of traditional clothing styles, such as the use of a kimono for the character of Ares, gives the film a global feel and adds to the sense that the characters inhabit a unique and complex world. The attention to detail in the costume design extends even to the accessories used in the film, such as the distinctive gold coins that are used as currency in the criminal underworld.

Another important aspect of the costume design in John Wick is the use of practical and functional clothing. John Wick's suits are tailored to allow him to move freely and perform the intricate fight choreography without hindrance. This attention to practicality extends to the other characters in the film as well, with many of the clothing choices reflecting the physical demands of their roles.

The costume design in John Wick is also notable for the use of subtle details and visual motifs. For example, John Wick's suit is often seen with a small bullet hole near the heart, a visual reminder of his past and the violence that drives him. Additionally, the use of the color blue in the film is often associated with memories of John's deceased wife and adds an emotional depth to the film's action sequences.

The costume design in John Wick plays a significant role in creating a unique and immersive world for the audience. The attention to detail and practicality in the design not only serves to enhance the film's action sequences but also adds to the characterization of the various characters in the film's criminal underworld. The use of subtle details and visual motifs also adds a layer of depth to the film's storytelling, making it a standout in the action genre.

# THE POWER DYNAMICS OF THE HIGH TABLE

The High Table is the governing body of the criminal underworld in the John Wick universe. It holds immense power and influence over the assassins and their organizations. In this chapter, we will examine the power dynamics of the High Table and how it affects the characters and events in the films.

Firstly, it is important to understand the structure of the High Table. It is comprised of twelve members who have absolute control over the assassins and their organizations. They have their own enforcers, known as Adjudicators, who ensure that their rules are followed and any transgressions are punished accordingly. The members are also expected to follow a strict code of conduct, which includes offering a marker to someone who has done them a favor, as we discussed in an earlier chapter.

One of the key aspects of the High Table's power is their ability to excommunicate someone from the world of assassins. This means that the person is effectively cut off from all the resources and support that they would normally have as an assassin. They become a target for anyone who wishes to kill them and are forced to go into hiding. We see this happen to John Wick in the first film after he breaks the rules by killing a member of the High Table on Continental grounds.

Another important aspect of the High Table's power is their ability to control the flow of resources. They have access to an immense amount of wealth, and they can use this to manipulate people and events in their favor. They control the gold coins, the currency of the assassin world, and can use them to buy loyalty or services.

They also have control over the Continental hotels, which provide a safe haven for assassins and are an important resource for anyone in the business.

The power dynamics of the High Table are also influenced by the personal relationships between the members. While they all have a shared interest in maintaining their power and influence, they are not always in agreement about how this should be achieved. We see this in the conflict between Winston and the Adjudicator in John Wick: Chapter 3 - Parabellum. Winston is the manager of the Continental in New York and has a close relationship with John Wick, which complicates his position when the Adjudicator comes to town. The Adjudicator accuses Winston of breaking the rules and threatens to take away his power, which forces him to make a difficult decision.

The High Table's power is also shown through their influence over the world outside of the assassin community. They have connections to the government, the police, and other organizations, which they can use to their advantage. This is shown in John Wick: Chapter 2, where John has to assassinate Gianna D'Antonio, a member of the High Table. He goes to Rome to carry out the job and finds himself caught up in a web of political intrigue and power struggles that extend far beyond the world of assassins.

The power dynamics of the High Table are an important aspect of the John Wick universe. They are a powerful and influential organization that controls the assassin world and has connections to other organizations outside of it. Their ability to control resources, manipulate events, and excommunicate people makes them a formidable force to be reckoned with. The conflicts between the members and the personal relationships between them add depth and complexity to the world, and provide a rich source of material for future films.

# AN EXPLORATION OF THE UNDERWORLD ECONOMY IN JOHN WICK

One of the most intriguing aspects of the John Wick universe is the complex and intricate underworld economy that operates within it. From the gold coins used to purchase goods and services, to the various criminal organizations that control different parts of the economy, the film provides a unique insight into a world that operates outside of conventional society. This chapter will explore the various aspects of the underworld economy in John Wick and how they contribute to the film's themes and overall aesthetic.

The gold coins are one of the most iconic aspects of the John Wick universe, serving as the primary currency used in the underworld economy. These coins have a specific weight and design, making them easily recognizable to those within the criminal underworld. In the film, we see John Wick use these coins to purchase a wide range of items, from guns to medical attention. But the use of gold coins as currency is not just a plot device – it serves to create a sense of history and tradition within the world of the film, hinting at a long-standing criminal society that operates according to its own set of rules.

Another fascinating aspect of the underworld economy in John Wick is the hierarchy of power that exists between different criminal organizations. At the top of this hierarchy is the High Table, a powerful organization that controls many aspects of the criminal underworld, including the assassins that operate within it. The High Table maintains its power through a series of strict rules and codes of conduct that all members of the underworld must adhere to. The consequences of breaking these rules can be severe, as we see when John Wick is excommunicated from the underworld for killing a member of the High Table.

Beyond the High Table, there are several other criminal organizations that operate within the underworld economy of John Wick. These organizations control different parts of the economy, from weapons manufacturing to the hotel industry. Each organization has its own set of rules and codes of conduct, and they all have a unique relationship with John Wick and his allies.

The role of the Continental Hotel in the underworld economy is also significant. The hotel serves as a neutral ground where members of the criminal underworld can meet and conduct business without fear of violence. It is also a place where assassins can rest and recuperate between jobs, making it an essential part of the underworld economy. The Continental Hotel is owned and operated by Winston, a powerful figure in the criminal underworld and a close ally of John Wick. The relationship between John Wick and Winston is one of the most fascinating aspects of the film, and the hotel serves as a backdrop for many important moments in the story.

The underworld economy in John Wick is a complex and multifaceted system that operates according to its own set of rules and traditions. It serves as an important backdrop for the film's themes of loyalty, honor, and revenge, and adds a layer of depth to the world of the film. Through the use of gold coins, powerful criminal organizations, and the Continental Hotel, the film creates a unique and immersive world that is both fascinating and terrifying. As viewers, we are drawn into this world and are left wanting to know more about its inner workings, making it an essential part of the overall John Wick experience.

# JOHN WICK AND THE ART OF ASSASSINATION

In the film John Wick, the titular character is known as the world's deadliest assassin. Throughout the movie, we see him execute intricate and highly choreographed kill sequences with seemingly effortless precision. But what exactly goes into the art of assassination in the John Wick universe?

One of the most prominent aspects of John Wick's assassination technique is his use of firearms. In the film, he is shown to be highly skilled in a variety of different weapons, from pistols to shotguns to assault rifles. But it's not just the weapons themselves that make him deadly - it's the way he uses them. John Wick is known for his accuracy and efficiency, taking out targets with a minimal amount of wasted movement or ammunition. This is especially evident in the film's iconic nightclub scene, in which Wick takes on a small army of henchmen with nothing but his trusty pistol and some expertly-timed headshots.

But it's not just about the guns. John Wick is also highly trained in hand-to-hand combat, as we see in his fights with other assassins throughout the film. These scenes are heavily influenced by martial arts films, with Wick utilizing techniques from Judo, Brazilian Jiu-Jitsu, and Muay Thai, among others. The result is a highly stylized and visually impressive fight sequence that is as much about the art of combat as it is about killing.

Another key element of John Wick's assassination technique is his use of strategy and tactics. He is always thinking several steps ahead, planning his moves and anticipating his opponent's reactions. This is evident in his use of distractions, misdirection, and clever use of his environment to gain the upper hand. For example, in the film's climactic fight scene, he uses his knowledge of the Continental Hotel's rules to take out his targets while avoiding detection.

Finally, there is the question of motivation. John Wick is not just killing for the sake of killing - he has a clear goal in mind, whether it's avenging his dead wife or seeking justice for his murdered dog. This gives his assassinations a sense of purpose and emotional weight that elevates them beyond mere violence.

In many ways, John Wick's approach to assassination is a reflection of the film's overall style and tone. It's highly stylized, with a focus on precision, efficiency, and strategy. But it's also brutal and uncompromising, with a clear sense of the consequences of violence. It's a unique blend of action movie tropes and art-house sensibilities that has resonated with audiences around the world.

The art of assassination in John Wick is a complex and multifaceted subject that touches on everything from weapons proficiency to martial arts technique to strategic thinking. But at its core, it's about creating a character who is both deadly and compelling, a modern-day samurai whose skills and code of honor make him a force to be reckoned with. It's this combination of style and substance that has made John Wick one of the most iconic action movie characters of the 21st century.

# THE ROLE OF DOGS IN JOHN WICK'S STORY

The use of dogs in the John Wick franchise is one of its most iconic and unique features. From the beginning of the first film, the audience sees John's deep connection to his dog, Daisy, and the lengths he will go to avenge her death. In this chapter, we will explore the role of dogs in John Wick's story, and the symbolism behind their presence in the films.

In John Wick, dogs play a crucial role in the plot. Daisy's murder is the catalyst for John's revenge spree, as it is the one thing that brings him back into the world he left behind. Her death not only fuels John's quest for vengeance but also serves as a symbol for his lost innocence and the life he left behind.

Beyond Daisy, dogs play an important role in the franchise's action sequences. In John Wick: Chapter 3 - Parabellum, the two Belgian Malinois dogs that are part of Halle Berry's character's entourage become key players in the film's climactic action sequence. Their highly trained abilities and intense loyalty to their owner add an extra layer of excitement and intensity to the already thrilling fight scenes.

But the use of dogs in John Wick is not just for action scenes and plot devices. The presence of dogs is also symbolic of John's character. John Wick is a man of few words, but his connection to his dogs shows his softer side. The dogs serve as a reminder that despite his reputation as the Baba Yaga, John is still capable of love and compassion.

The franchise also uses dogs to contrast John's character with those of his enemies. While John's dogs are symbols of loyalty and companionship, his enemies use dogs as tools for their nefarious schemes. In John Wick: Chapter 2, we see that Santino D'Antonio, one of John's enemies, uses his dog to taunt and intimidate John. This contrast highlights the different values and morals that exist in the world of John Wick.

the use of dogs in John Wick is a unique and effective storytelling tool. They serve as plot devices, action scene enhancers, and symbols of John's character. The franchise's commitment to featuring highly trained dogs and incorporating them into the action sequences adds a level of excitement that is rare in other action films. Furthermore, their presence creates a contrast between John's character and his enemies, highlighting the different values that exist in this world.

The role of dogs in John Wick's story is significant and multifaceted. From plot devices to symbols of character, their presence adds depth and meaning to the films. The franchise's commitment to using highly trained dogs and incorporating them into the action sequences makes John Wick unique among other action films. the use of dogs is just one of the many elements that make John Wick a thrilling and complex cinematic experience.

# THE USE OF SLOW MOTION IN JOHN WICK'S ACTION SCENES

The use of slow motion in John Wick's action scenes has become one of the defining characteristics of the franchise's style. This technique not only makes the fight scenes more visually striking, but it also serves a storytelling purpose. In this chapter, we will explore the significance and impact of slow motion in John Wick's action scenes.

Firstly, slow motion allows the audience to fully appreciate the choreography and skill of the performers. It provides a moment of clarity amidst the chaos of the fight. It also emphasizes the physicality of the fights and the brutality of the violence, as we see the impact of each blow in detail. This is especially important in a film like John Wick, where the action is the primary draw for audiences.

Additionally, slow motion can be used to heighten the tension and suspense in a scene. By slowing down the action, the filmmakers can draw out a moment and create anticipation for what will happen next. For example, in John Wick: Chapter 3 - Parabellum, there is a sequence where Wick is pursued by a team of assassins on motorcycles. The slow-motion shots of the motorcycles approaching, combined with the sound of their engines revving, creates a sense of impending danger that keeps the audience on the edge of their seats.

Moreover, slow motion can also be used to convey emotion and character development. In John Wick's fight scenes, slow motion often emphasizes his determination and will to survive. We see the exhaustion and pain in his face as he continues to fight, and the slow-motion shots of his battered body and bloody wounds serve as a reminder of the toll his actions take on him. This adds depth to his character and makes him more relatable to the audience.

Finally, slow motion can also serve a narrative purpose. It can be used to reveal important information or to highlight key moments in the story. For example, in John Wick: Chapter 2, there is a sequence where Wick is fighting his way through a crowded subway station. The slow-motion shots of the other commuters going about their daily lives amidst the chaos of the fight convey the idea that the world of the assassins exists alongside our own, but is hidden from view. This adds to the film's world-building and enhances the sense of immersion for the audience.

Slow motion is a powerful tool in John Wick's action scenes, providing both visual spectacle and narrative depth. Its use enhances the impact of the fights, creates tension and suspense, conveys emotion and character development, and serves a narrative purpose. The combination of expert choreography, intense performances, and stylish direction makes John Wick's slow-motion action scenes some of the most memorable in recent cinema.

# AN ANALYSIS OF THE CINEMATOGRAPHY IN JOHN WICK

The success of the John Wick franchise can be attributed to various factors, such as the compelling storyline, the intense action sequences, and the incredible performances by the actors. However, one aspect that often goes unnoticed is the impressive cinematography that is evident throughout the films. The cinematography in John Wick plays a significant role in creating the mood and atmosphere of the film, capturing the nuances of the characters' emotions and highlighting the brutality of the action scenes. This chapter will provide an in-depth analysis of the cinematography in John Wick.

One of the most striking features of the cinematography in John Wick is the use of color grading. The film's color palette consists mainly of blue and yellow hues, which create a cold and sterile atmosphere that is consistent with the film's setting. The color grading also helps to emphasize the violence in the film, making the blood and gore stand out against the cool-toned backgrounds. Furthermore, the use of color grading also provides a contrast between the criminal underworld and the ordinary world, as seen in the bright and warm colors of the suburban areas.

Another significant aspect of the cinematography in John Wick is the use of long takes. Long takes are unbroken shots that can last for several minutes, providing an uninterrupted view of the action. In John Wick, the long takes are used to capture the intense and brutal fight scenes, highlighting the skill and choreography of the actors and the stunt team. These long takes create a sense of tension and urgency, as the audience is kept on edge as they watch the action unfold.

In addition to long takes, John Wick also uses handheld camera shots to create a sense of immediacy and intimacy. Handheld shots are often used in close combat scenes, providing a shaky and frenetic feel to the action. These shots help to immerse the audience in the fight scenes, creating a sense of chaos and disorientation that is consistent with the chaos of the criminal underworld.

John Wick also makes use of different camera angles to provide different perspectives on the action. For example, low-angle shots are used to create a sense of power and dominance, highlighting the strength of the characters and their skill in combat. Conversely, high-angle shots are used to create a sense of vulnerability and weakness, highlighting the danger that the characters face. These different camera angles help to create a sense of depth and dimensionality to the action, making the audience feel like they are part of the scene.

Finally, John Wick also makes use of visual motifs and symbolism to reinforce the themes and ideas of the film. For example, the use of mirrors and reflections is prevalent throughout the film, highlighting the duality of the characters and the contrast between the criminal underworld and the ordinary world. The use of light and shadow is also prominent, creating a sense of mystery and danger in the scenes.

The cinematography in John Wick is a crucial component of the film's success. The use of color grading, long takes, handheld shots, camera angles, and visual motifs all contribute to the film's atmosphere and tone, making it a unique and engaging cinematic experience. Through careful analysis, it is evident that the cinematography in John Wick is a masterful work of art that deserves recognition and appreciation.

# THE INFLUENCE OF JAPANESE SAMURAI FILMS ON JOHN WICK

John Wick is a movie that draws inspiration from a wide range of cinematic sources. One of the most significant influences on the film is Japanese Samurai cinema. From the aesthetic of the characters' clothing to the use of certain fighting techniques, the influence of Samurai films is evident throughout John Wick.

One of the most obvious connections between John Wick and Samurai cinema is the use of the katana sword. The katana is a weapon closely associated with the Samurai, and it is prominently featured in several fight scenes in the film. The way in which John Wick wields the katana is also reminiscent of Samurai fighting techniques, particularly the way in which he holds the weapon with both hands and uses swift, precise movements to strike his opponents.

Another way in which John Wick pays homage to Samurai cinema is through its use of clothing and costume design. The suits worn by the characters in John Wick are not just any ordinary suits. They are designed to be functional, allowing the characters to move freely and quickly during action sequences. The sharp lines and minimalist style of the suits also call to mind the sleek and elegant clothing worn by Samurai warriors.

The use of color in John Wick is another nod to Japanese Samurai cinema. The film makes prominent use of the color red, which is traditionally associated with Samurai culture. Red is used in the film to signify danger and death, as well as to create a sense of visual contrast in the action scenes.

The use of Japanese terminology and culture in John Wick is also evidence of the film's influence from Samurai cinema. For example, the term "ronin" is used to describe John Wick, and the film's criminal underworld is referred to as the "Yakuza." The use of these terms adds a layer of cultural depth to the film, and serves to connect it to the wider tradition of Japanese cinema.

Finally, John Wick's portrayal of honor and respect is another hallmark of Samurai cinema. The film's titular character is a man who values his word and holds true to his code, much like a Samurai warrior. He is also shown to have a deep respect for his opponents, even as he dispatches them with deadly force.

John Wick draws heavily on the rich tradition of Japanese Samurai cinema. From the use of the katana sword to the influence on costume design and color, the film is infused with elements of this cinematic tradition. This connection to Samurai cinema adds a layer of cultural depth and richness to the film, and helps to make John Wick a truly unique and memorable action movie experience.

# THE ROLE OF SOUND DESIGN IN JOHN WICK'S ACTION SCENES

The action scenes in John Wick are some of the most thrilling and intense in recent cinema, and much of this is due to the film's excellent sound design. From the sounds of gunshots and explosions to the crunch of bones breaking and the swish of knives cutting through the air, every sound in John Wick's world is carefully crafted to enhance the impact of the action.

In this chapter, we will explore the role of sound design in John Wick's action scenes and how it contributes to the film's overall style and tone. We will examine the techniques used by sound designer Martín Hernández to create the film's immersive soundscapes, as well as the ways in which the sound design works in tandem with the film's other elements, such as the cinematography and music.

One of the key aspects of the sound design in John Wick is the use of realistic and visceral sounds. The film's sound team went to great lengths to capture the sounds of real guns and other weapons being fired, resulting in a sense of authenticity that adds to the film's realism. The sounds of impacts, such as punches and kicks, are also carefully crafted to create a visceral impact, with foley artists using a variety of techniques to create the desired sounds, including breaking celery and smashing melons.

Another important element of the sound design in John Wick is the use of dynamic range. The film employs a wide range of volume levels, from quiet moments of dialogue to deafening explosions, creating a sense of tension and excitement. This dynamic range is particularly effective in the film's action scenes, where the sudden shift from quiet to loud can be jarring and thrilling.

In addition to creating a sense of realism and excitement, the sound design in John Wick also serves to enhance the film's style and tone. The use of specific sounds, such as the ominous sound of the Continental Hotel's bell, creates a sense of atmosphere and adds to the film's noir-inspired aesthetic. The use of music, both diegetic and non-diegetic, also contributes to the film's overall sound design, with composer Tyler Bates' score and the film's use of popular songs adding to the sense of energy and excitement.

Finally, we will also examine the ways in which the sound design in John Wick is used to enhance the emotional impact of the film's key moments. The use of silence, for example, can be just as powerful as the use of sound, and the film's sound team is careful to use both to great effect. The sound design is also used to create a sense of isolation and disorientation, such as in the film's climactic battle in the hall of mirrors.

The sound design in John Wick is a masterclass in the art of creating immersive and impactful soundscapes. By carefully crafting every sound in the film's world, the sound team has helped to create a film that is both thrilling and emotionally engaging. Whether you're a fan of action films or simply appreciate the art of sound design, there is much to be learned and appreciated from the sound of John Wick.

# THE ETHICS OF KILLING IN JOHN WICK

The John Wick franchise is known for its intense and stylized action scenes, but at its core, it raises important questions about the ethics of killing. The central character, John Wick, is an assassin who has left his violent past behind, but is inevitably pulled back into the world of organized crime. The film explores the idea of whether it is ever justifiable to take another person's life and what it means to live with the consequences of one's actions.

Throughout the films, John Wick is often portrayed as a sympathetic character, despite the fact that he is a highly trained killer. This is in part due to his tragic backstory, which includes the loss of his wife and beloved dog, but it also raises questions about the nature of justice and revenge. When is it okay to seek revenge and when does it cross the line into becoming an act of vigilantism?

The films also raise important questions about the value of human life. In the world of John Wick, people are often killed for the slightest offense or perceived disrespect. The fact that the violence is portrayed in such a stylized and glamorous way raises questions about whether or not it is being glorified, and whether or not it is sending the wrong message to audiences.

One of the most interesting aspects of the John Wick films is the way they explore the idea of redemption. Despite his violent past, John Wick is presented as a sympathetic character who is trying to make amends for his past actions. This raises questions about whether or not people can truly change, and whether or not society should be willing to forgive and forget past misdeeds.

The films also explore the idea of duty and loyalty. John Wick is bound by a code of honor and a sense of duty to those he has made commitments to. This raises questions about whether or not loyalty to a person or an organization can ever justify taking another person's life.

Finally, the films also explore the idea of the cost of violence. John Wick is a highly skilled killer, but he is not immune to the physical and emotional toll that his actions take on him. The films show the toll that violence takes on both the victims and the perpetrators, and raise important questions about whether or not the ends ever truly justify the means.

The ethics of killing is a central theme in the John Wick franchise. The films explore a range of complex and challenging questions about the nature of justice, revenge, loyalty, and redemption. Through the character of John Wick, the films invite audiences to consider the cost of violence and to question the glamorization of killing in popular culture.

# JOHN WICK'S IMPACT ON ACTION FILM GENRE

John Wick, the stylish and violent action movie series, has received critical and commercial success, becoming a modern icon of the genre. Its innovative action sequences, captivating cinematography, and intriguing world-building have brought the franchise to the forefront of action filmmaking. This chapter will explore the impact John Wick has had on the action film genre.

## THE REBIRTH OF PRACTICAL EFFECTS:

One of the most significant impacts of John Wick on action films is the return to practical effects. John Wick's action scenes are known for their realistic choreography, and the use of practical effects instead of CGI has resulted in a heightened sense of authenticity. This trend has been echoed in other action movies such as Mad Max: Fury Road and the Mission Impossible series, demonstrating the influence of John Wick.

## THE EMERGENCE OF THE GUN-FU SUBGENRE:

John Wick introduced a new subgenre of action films called gun-fu, a style that combines martial arts and gunplay. The choreography is incredibly fast-paced, and the result is an intense and thrilling viewing experience. This style has influenced other movies such as Atomic Blonde, The Equalizer, and Gunpowder Milkshake, cementing John Wick's place in the action genre.

### THE RISE OF WORLD-BUILDING:

John Wick's unique world-building, where assassins have their own hidden society with strict rules and regulations, has had a significant impact on the action film genre. The movies' success has shown that audiences are interested in exploring richly detailed and intricate worlds. Other films, such as Extraction and Nobody, have followed in John Wick's footsteps, creating complex worlds that are ripe for exploration.

### THE IMPORTANCE OF CHARACTER DEVELOPMENT:

The John Wick franchise is known for its nuanced character development, particularly for its titular character. The films don't just rely on action sequences to tell the story, but also on the emotional depth of its characters. This approach has been influential in the action genre, leading to movies such as The Old Guard and Nobody, which feature well-developed and complex characters.

### THE TREND TOWARDS R-RATED ACTION FILMS:

John Wick's success has proven that R-rated action films can be both financially successful and critically acclaimed. This has led to a trend towards more adult-oriented action movies, with other films such as Deadpool and Logan also achieving similar success. John Wick's influence has shown that action films don't have to be formulaic and safe to appeal to a wide audience.

The John Wick franchise has had a significant impact on the action film genre, from the use of practical effects and the emergence of gun-fu to the importance of world-building and character development. Its success has led to a renewed interest in R-rated action movies that prioritize action and storytelling over flashy CGI effects. John Wick's impact on the genre is undeniable, and its legacy will continue to shape the future of action filmmaking.

# ABOUT ETERNIA PUBLISHING

This guide is a result of thorough research from various official sources, including books, courses, biographies, and interviews by renowned experts in the respective fields.

The content is presented in a simplified and practical manner, leaving out redundancies, unnecessary and irrelevant information, and only focusing on the key concepts.

The sources of knowledge are carefully selected and relevant, and the guide aims to provide a broad overview of the reader's topics of interest.

The ultimate goal is to ensure that the text is easily understandable, practical, and pleasant to read.

The reader can acquire a large amount of knowledge from more than one reliable source, making it a useful resource.

The guide is designed to help readers learn and understand specialized information with the greatest effectiveness.

# COPYRIGHT

This book is protected by copyright, and it is not allowed to reproduce its content in whole or in part without written permission from the author and/or publisher.

Quotes used in reviews or critical articles must be credited to the source, including the book title, edition, author, publisher, and publication date.

Any form of reproduction, duplication, or distribution, including photocopying, scanning, downloading, recording, and translating, is prohibited without written consent, except for citations in reviews or criticism. The publisher and author recognize the original book's copyright.

The book aims to provide accurate information, but the publisher is not responsible for providing qualified services on the subject. It is the reader's responsibility to interpret the content and use it responsibly.

# LEGAL DISCLAIMER

This book aims to provide information and entertainment to its readers. The author has used reliable sources for the content, but cannot guarantee its accuracy or validity and is not responsible for any errors or omissions.

The book is not intended to be professional advice and should not replace the guidance of experts. The reader should consult professionals before using any protocols or medical treatments described in the book.

The reader agrees to use the information in the book at their own risk and the author is not liable for any costs, expenses, damages, or professional fees that may arise from using the information in the book. This disclaimer applies to any direct or indirect use of the information, and the author is not liable for any damages, negligence, criminal intent or other causes of action.

# REVIEWS

We hope that this book has been helpful in providing a deeper understanding and analysis of the subject.

We appreciate your time in reading and hope that you found the content useful.

If you enjoyed the book, we would be grateful if you could leave a positive review, as this is one of the ways for new authors like us to gain visibility and improve the quality of our writing.

Thank you for your support!

Unveiling John Wick: Unleashing The Baba Yaga: An In-Depth
Analysis And Anatomy Of A Modern Action Hero
By Eternia Publishing and Zander Pearce



Author: Eternia Publishing and Zander Pearce
Contact: contact@eterniapublishing.com

www.ingramcontent.com/pod-product-compliance
Lightning Source LLC
Chambersburg PA
CBHW052115150726
48002CB00006B/2365